This is My Pet!

Helen Chapman

Contents

Look at Our Pets

Look at our pets!

They are not dogs.
They are not cats.

Stick insect

This is my pet.
She has thin legs.
She looks like a stick.

My pet is
a stick insect.

This is my pet.
My pet has big ears.
But he is little!

My pet is
a mini donkey.

Ferret

This is my pet.
She is long and thin.
She has short legs.

My pet is a ferret.

Mini Turtle

This is my pet.
She has a hard shell.
She likes to swim.

My pet is
a mini turtle.

Spider

This is my pet.
He has lots of legs.
He likes to eat mice.

My pet is a tarantula.

Walking Fish

This is my pet.
My pet looks like a fish.
But he can walk on land!

My pet is
a Mexican walking
fish.

Picture index